Hello Dad

Finding your father and getting to know him

Hello Dad

Finding your father and getting to know him

by

Karen Bali

Published by WritersPrintshop

www.people-search.co.uk

First published in Great Britain 2004
by WritersPrintshop

ISBN 1904623107

Designed by
Rob Oldfield Design Associates

Disclaimer
The author has attempted to produce a text for use in
personal research and all information within is available to
the general public. Instructions for use are guidelines only.
The author is not responsible for any legal information
within this publication, which may change at any time.
Also, no responsibility can be held by the author or
publisher for any misuse of information within the text.

Contents

Acknowledgements
There are many people to thank for making this book possible. Hugh Graham, for his encouragement and guidance, Fiona Hibberd from Lloyds TSB for her help with business and project planning, David Sims-Mindry for believing in People Search, Les Willson and Steve Cole for the technical stuff, Barbara Williams, Sharon Ross and Heather White for being the best friends in the world, many generous clients who have shared their personal experiences and of course my wonderful family – my darling husband Sunil, daughter Sitara and son Ashwin – you are the best.

List of plates

Introduction

More than 30 percent of People Search enquiries start with the words 'I want to find my father'. After four years, and with the number of requests increasing, the idea for this book began to take shape. Realising that I can never possibly help everyone who feels the need to search for their father, it is hoped that this book will cover many of the questions people have and provide some of the answers.

Why so many missing fathers?

Until the middle of the 20th century, almost all children were born to married couples that remained together. By 1971, just over 8 percent of births were to single mothers and by 2001 this figure had increased to 40 percent.

At the same time, divorce was becoming increasingly common. In 1991 there were more than five times the number of divorces than in 1951, so even children born to married parents are more likely to end up living with only one parent – usually their mother. Single parent families made up just 6 percent of households in the early 1970s but this figure had risen to almost 20 percent by the year 2000.

A survey of single mothers in 1999 asked about their children's relationships with their former husbands or partners. Around one third said that there was no contact between children and fathers and one fifth did not know where the fathers were living. As the average number of children born each year is currently around 600,000, this suggests that potentially millions of young people reaching adulthood in the coming decades will have no contact with their father*.

Why don't fathers keep in touch?

Although it can seem personal and feel like rejection, the reasons why fathers do not keep in touch with their children vary a great deal. It is not always that they can't be bothered or do not love the child. This may be the case with a small number of course, but often the reasons are more complex. Where men have witnessed the birth of their baby, have been in a stable relationship with the mother or lived in the same household with the child for some time, a bond of affection usually means that the father keeps in touch even after the partnership or marriage breaks down. The fact that a child is their biological offspring is not always sufficient reason for the father to make the effort to remain in touch.

There are of course many cases where fathers, despite having almost no contact with the child from birth, will fight to stay in touch, have the child to visit and develop a close and loving relationship. One father tried to explain why he continued contact with his teenage son but never saw the boy's younger sister. He said that by the time his marriage broke down, his son was almost five and he had already become 'very fond of him', but his daughter was just a baby, born after the split. He felt that he did not know his daughter at all and felt that as his ex-wife was remarried he should 'leave things be'.

Hostility between the parents and an acrimonious split is more likely than anything else to result in loss of contact between father and child.

A new wife also brings another person into the equation, someone else to consider, and often a new relationship can take priority. Occasionally the second or subsequent wife will make it known that she would not welcome children from a previous relationship or want her partner to give attention only to children they have together. Children of second or subsequent marriages are not always told about half brothers and sisters, the parents feeling that it's best they don't know, so contact with the children of the first relationship is not sought or maintained. Sometimes, however, a stepmother will suggest or encourage contact with other children.

When thinking about this type of search, many fear that their father will assume they want money. They may spell out in length that they 'do not want anything from him'. In my experience this is almost never an issue for the father, however.

How this book can help

Firstly, it can help to feel that you are not alone. There are many thousands of others in the country who do not know or have no contact their father. It is easy to feel isolated when people around you have two loving parents and the media is full of 'happy family' images.

Secondly, on a practical level, there is help with research and tracing your father. There is also advice on making an approach to him in a considered and responsible way, to minimise the chance of sabotaging the new relationship before it has begun.

The emotional process is discussed and what to expect at every step of the way. This includes dealing with other family members and how they may be affected.

Finally, real case histories show how each search, and the outcome, is different. The reasons, the process, the approach and the reaction makes every case unique.

Before you start

You may want to start the search as soon as you make the decision to look for your father. It will help a great deal if you first take a little time to reflect on the reasons for your search. Some say that it is just curiosity, others need medical information or would like to know what their father looks like. Many people who undertake a search of this nature, however, describe a feeling of 'something missing'. Reading the case histories in Chapter 7 will show that not all searches end 'happily ever after'. Before making contact it is usually helpful to think about your hopes and expectations. It can happen that getting carried away with the search can lead you to make contact before any thought has been given to what it is you really want. Giving yourself time to consider this, and preferably to also talk it through with a partner, relative or trusted friend, is the very best way to start a search.

Wishing you the best of luck with yours.
Sincerely,
Karen Bali
People Search Tracing Services, 2004
*All figures from National Statistics at www.statistics.gov.uk

Chapter One

Tracing your father

When you haven't seen your father since you were a child, how do you start looking for him? Where and how you start the search depends on how much information you have about him and his family.

Ask yourself the following questions then make a list of everything you know about him.

- Were my parents married and if so where and when?
- Did my parents live together at the time of my birth?
- Is my father's name on my birth certificate?
- What was his occupation?
- How old is he?
- Who were his parents, brothers, sisters, and close friends?
- When did he and my mother lose touch?
- What was his last known address/location?

Start with your birth certificate
Your birth certificate may be the most valuable clue to starting out on the search for your father. If you have a copy of your full birth certificate, get it out and take a look. It will either be an 'old style' landscape certificate or one of the newer ones in a portrait layout, which contains a little more information about both parents.

These birth certificates are examples of both styles, showing the information you will find on each.

Example A

SPECIMEN

CERTIFIED COPY
Pursuant to the Births and
of an ENTRY
Deaths Registration Act 1953

FC 000077

Registration District Southport

Birth in the Sub-district of Southport in the County of Lancashire

1955.

Columns:-	1	2	3	4	5	6	7	8	9	10
No.	When and where born	Name, if any	Sex	Name, and surname of father	Name, surname and maiden surname of mother	Occupation of father	Signature, description, and residence of informant	When registered	Signature of registrar	Name entered after registration
194	Sixth July, 1955 Manor House, Southport	Mary Helen	Girl	Thomas Milner	Isabella Milner, formerly Watkins of 11 Long Lane, Southport	Land Owner	Thomas Milner, Father, 11 Long Lane, Southport	Tenth July, 1955	L. McMahon Registrar	

Certified to be a true copy of an entry in a register in my custody.

WARNING: A CERTIFICATE IS NOT EVIDENCE OF IDENTITY.

CAUTION: THERE ARE OFFENCES RELATING TO FALSIFYING OR ALTERING A CERTIFICATE AND USING OR POSSESSING A FALSE CERTIFICATE. ©CROWN COPYRIGHT

Office for National Statistics © Crown copyright.
Reproduced with the permission of the Controller of HMSO

If your parents were married to each other at the time of your birth, your certificate will be similar to **A** or **B**:

A will show the full name of your father, his occupation and the family address at the time of your birth.

B will show his full name, occupation, address and also his place of birth.

If you have a certificate similar to **A** or **B** you have an excellent chance of finding your father.

Hello Dad - Finding your Father

Example B

SPECIMEN
CERTIFIED COPY OF AN ENTRY
Pursuant to the Births and Deaths Registration Act 1953

BD 355561

BIRTH | Entry No. 13

Registration district Sefton North	Administrative area
Sub-district Sefton North	County of Sefton

1. Date and place of birth **CHILD**
Seventeenth May 2003
Woodlands Nursing Home, Birkdale

2. Name and surname Bonnie CHARNWOOD	**3. Sex** Female

4. Name and surname **FATHER**
Andrew Raymond CHARNWOOD

5. Place of birth Mevigissy, Cornwall	**6.** Occupation Solicitor

7. Name and surname **MOTHER**
Susan Jane CHARNWOOD

8.(a) Place of birth Crewe, Cheshire	**8.(b)** Occupation Interior Designer
9.(a) Maiden surname GREAVES	**9.(b)** Surname at marriage if different from maiden surname ....

10. Usual address (if different from place of child's birth)
6 Hastings Road, Birkdale, Southport

11. Name and surname (if not the mother or father) **INFORMANT**	**12.** Qualification Father

13. Usual address
(if different from
that in 10 above)

14. I certify that the particulars entered above are true to the best of my knowledge and belief
A Charnwood

Signature
of informant

15. Date of registration Third June 2003	**16.** Signature of registrar Liz McMahon Registrar

17. Name given
after registration,
and surname

Certified to be a true copy of an entry in a register in my custody.

.... {   *Superintendent Registrar.   Date 6/6/2003
                                        *Registrar
                                        *delete that which does not apply

CAUTION: THERE ARE OFFENCES RELATING TO FALSIFYING OR ALTERING A CERTIFICATE AND USING
OR POSSESSING A FALSE CERTIFICATE. ©CROWN COPYRIGHT.
WARNING: A CERTIFICATE IS NOT EVIDENCE OF IDENTITY.

Office for National Statistics © Crown copyright.
Reproduced with the permission of the Controller of HMSO

*If your parents were married to each other at the time of your birth and your certificate is similar to **A** or **B**, the most accurate and cost effective way to trace your father will probably be through a non-profit making agency – Traceline (England and Wales only) or the Salvation Army Family Tracing Service – see information later in this chapter.*

Example C

SPECIMEN

FC 000079

CERTIFIED COPY of an ENTRY
Pursuant to the Births and Deaths Registration Act 1953

Registration District Southport

Birth in the Sub-district of Southport in the County of Lancashire

No.	When and where born	Name, if any	Sex	Name, and surname of father	Name, surname and maiden surname of mother	Occupation of father	Signature, description, and residence of informant	When registered	Signature of registrar	Name entered after registration
98	Twenty-fifth September, 1955 The Market Tavern, 10, Main Road, Southport	Pamela	Girl	William Henry Jones	Henrietta Morris of 10 Eltham Place, Churchtown	Draper's Assistant	W. H. Jones, Father. 19 Fisher Street, Southport Henrietta Morris, Mother, 10 Eltham Place, Churchtown	Tenth October, 1955	L. McMahon Registrar	

Certified to be a true copy of an entry in a register in my custody.

WARNING: A CERTIFICATE IS NOT EVIDENCE OF IDENTITY.

CAUTION: IT IS AN OFFENCE TO FALSIFY A CERTIFICATE OR TO MAKE OR KNOWINGLY USE A FALSE CERTIFICATE OR A COPY OF A FALSE CERTIFICATE INTENDING IT TO BE ACCEPTED AS GENUINE TO THE PREJUDICE OF ANY PERSON, OR TO POSSESS A CERTIFICATE KNOWING IT TO BE FALSE WITHOUT LAWFUL AUTHORITY. FOR CROWN COPYRIGHT

Examples **C** and **D** show the birth of a child where the parents were not married to each other but both names are given. An unmarried woman cannot register the birth of her baby and give a man's details as the father of the child without him being present. If both parents' names are shown on your birth certificate, both would have been present at the time of registration. This suggests that they were perhaps in a steady relationship and that your father was prepared accept you were his child. They may have lived together as a couple, even for some time.

Example D

SPECIMEN
BD 355568

CERTIFIED COPY OF AN ENTRY

Pursuant to the Births and   Deaths Registration Act 1953

BIRTH	Entry No. 15

Registration district Sefton North

Administrative area
County of Sefton

Sub-district   Sefton North

CHILD

1. Date and place of birth
Twenty-ninth May 2003
Royal Infirmary, Southport

2. Name and surname
Penelope Jane CAVENDISH

3. Sex
Female

FATHER

4. Name and surname
Michael Richard CAVENDISH

5. Place of birth
New Zealand

6. Occupation
Dentist

MOTHER

7. Name and surname
Susan Lorna SMITH

8.(a) Place of birth
Warrington, Cheshire

8.(b) Occupation
Dental Nurse

9.(a) Maiden surname

9.(b) Surname at marriage if different from maiden surname

10. Usual address (if different from place of child's birth)
3 High Street, Southport

INFORMANT

11. Name and surname (if not the mother or father)

12. Qualification
Father
Mother

13. Usual address
(if different from
that in 10 above)   3 High Street, Southport

14. I certify that the particulars entered above are true to the best of my knowledge and belief
M Cavendish   S Smith

Signature
of informant

15. Date of registration
Third June 2003

16. Signature of registrar
Liz McMahon Registrar

17. Name given
after registration,
and surname

Certified to be a true copy of an entry in a register in my custody.

{ *Superintendent Registrar
*Registrar   Date 6/6/2003
*strike out whichever does not apply

CAUTION THERE ARE OFFENCES RELATING TO FALSIFYING OR ALTERING A CERTIFICATE AND USING
OR POSSESSING A FALSE CERTIFICATE. *CROWN COPYRIGHT

WARNING: A CERTIFICATE IS NOT EVIDENCE OF IDENTITY.

Office for National Statistics © Crown copyright.
Reproduced with the permission of the Controller of HMSO

The certificate will tell you whether or not your parents were living at the same address and your father's occupation. Certificates similar to **D** will also show his place of birth.

Traceline *will probably be able to help you, even if you parents were not married, so long as his name is on your birth certificate.*
The Salvation Army Family Tracing Service *will not conduct a search for your father if your parents were not married to each other.*

Example E

FC 000078

SPECIMEN

CERTIFIED COPY of an ENTRY
Pursuant to the Births and Deaths Registration Act 1953

Registration District Southport

Birth in the Sub-district of Southport in the County of Lancashire

Columns:	1	2	3	4	5	6	7	8	9	10
No.	When and where born	Name, if any	Sex	Name, and surname of father	Name, surname and maiden surname of mother	Occupation of father	Signature, description, and residence of informant	When registered	Signature of registrar	Name entered after registration
119	Fourth September, 1955 St. Stephens Hospital, Southport	William	Boy		Elizabeth Groves, a Cook (Domestic) of 3, High Street, Southport		Elizabeth Groves, Mother 3, High Street, Southport	Tenth October, 1955	L. McMahon Registrar	

Certified to be a true copy of an entry in a register in my custody.

CAUTION: THERE ARE OFFENCES RELATING TO FALSIFYING OR ALTERING A CERTIFICATE AND USING OR POSSESSING A FALSE CERTIFICATE. © CROWN COPYRIGHT.

WARNING: A CERTIFICATE IS NOT EVIDENCE OF IDENTITY.

Superintendent Registrar

6/5/2003 Date

Office for National Statistics © Crown copyright.

Many people reading this book, however, will have birth certificates similar to E or F. Certificates without the father's details are issued where the parents were not married to each other and the father was not present at the time of registration. This often, but not always, means that the mother had sole responsibility and that her relationship with the father was not long-term. Sometimes there is no tangible evidence of who your father is. However, there is often something that you have: a photograph, letters, legal documents, that might give more clues about him.

Example F

BIRTH	Entry No. 14

Registration district Sefton North	Administrative area
Sub-district Sefton North	County of Sefton

1. Date and place of birth	**CHILD**	

Twenty-second May 2003
Southport Maternity Hospital

2. Name and surname	3. Sex
Russell Henry BRIGSTOCK	Male

4. Name and surname	**FATHER**

5. Place of birth	6. Occupation

7. Name and surname	**MOTHER**
Ruth Pamela BRIGSTOCK	

8.(a) Place of birth	8.(b) Occupation
Preston, Lancashire	Hairdresser

9.(a) Maiden surname	9.(b) Surname at marriage if different from maiden surname

10. Usual address (if different from place of child's birth)
44 Seaview Crescent, Southport

11. Name and surname (if not the mother or father) **INFORMANT**	12. Qualification
	Mother

13. Usual address (if different from that in 10 above)

14. I certify that the particulars entered above are true to the best of my knowledge and belief	
R Brigstock	Signature of Informant

15. Date of registration	16. Signature of registrar
Third June 2003	Liz McMahon Registrar

17. Name given after registration, and surname

Certified to be a true copy of an entry in a register in my custody

.... {   Superintendent Registrar   Date 4/3/2003
    *Registrar

*Strike out whichever does not apply

CAUTION: THERE ARE OFFENCES RELATING TO FALSIFYING OR ALTERING A CERTIFICATE AND USING OR POSSESSING A FALSE CERTIFICATE. ©CROWN COPYRIGHT

WARNING: A CERTIFICATE IS NOT EVIDENCE OF IDENTITY.

N.B. *Traceline* can sometimes help, even if your father's name is not on your birth certificate, if you can provide proof that he is your father. Usually, this would need to be in the form of a solicitor's letter, maintenance papers or court documents. Contact *Traceline* for advice before commencing a lengthy search or paying money to a researcher or investigator.

How to obtain a copy of your birth certificate

If you do not have a copy of your birth certificate, you can obtain one either from the local register office in the district where your birth took place or from the General Register Office (hereafter called the GRO). You will need to supply detailed information including your full date of birth and your mother's full name (this is to stop someone else getting your birth certificate to use for fraudulent purposes).

District register offices and can usually be found in the telephone directory under 'Registration of Births, Deaths and Marriages'.

There are separate GRO departments for England and Wales, Scotland, and Northern Ireland.

Their contact details are as follows:

England and Wales
General Register Office
Smedley Hydro
Trafalgar Road
Southport PR8 2HH
Tel: 0870 243 7788
www.statistics.gov.uk/registration/general_register.asp

Scotland
New Register House
3 West Register Street
Edinburgh EH1 3YT
Tel: 0131 314 4411
www.gro-scotland.gov.uk

Northern Ireland
The General Register Office
Oxford House
49-55 Chichester Street
Belfast BT1 4HL
Tel (028) 90252000
www.groni.gov.uk/index.htm

Your mum

Sometimes, mothers are reluctant to talk about natural fathers, especially if the memories of the relationship or the way it ended are painful. Making demands out of the blue for information about your dad may come as a shock to her, so ask carefully. Mum is often your main, if not only, source of information so it's important to handle discussions with her well.

One good and valid reason for raising the subject is medical history. If nothing else, a medical history from both parents is valuable and can become more important as you get older or start to raise children of your own. Questions about medical history crop up when you develop an illness, undergo hospital treatment or have a baby. It can be frustrating to continually say that you know nothing about your father's health or the medical history of his family. At worst it could hinder treatment or mean that you neglect to have important genetic tests carried out. Put that way, even the most reluctant mothers might be persuaded to open up a little.

Relatives and Friends

If your mum is unwilling or unable to help, or if she is no longer around, other family members or close friends who knew her at the time of your birth may be able to come up with snippets of information about your father that will help in your search.

What to ask?

It's important to get your mum and others to think about your dad carefully and take their time trying to remember as much about him as possible. Encourage free conversation, but ask relevant questions to ensure that what you find out is useful. It may be nice to know that your dad had lovely brown eyes, had a passion for sports cars or could sing beautifully (or not so nice to hear that he was too fond of beer, got into fights and was always in debt). However, more useful is the identifying information that when put together provides the basis of your search.

This might be:
- Age
- Birthday
- Where he was born
- Where he was educated
- Occupation
- Ambitions

- Names of his parents, brothers or sisters
- Where his family lived and his father's occupation
- His last known address
- Whether he had been married
- Names of his close friends
- Connections with any other countries

Grandparents, aunts and uncles

If you have difficulty locating your father and you can find out the names of his parents, brothers or sisters, it may be possible to locate him through them. *Only consider this if your parents were married to each other or if you are sure that his family knows about you.*

Adopted persons

If you were adopted, either by another family, or by your natural mother and her new husband or partner, there should be a written note at the end or the bottom of the certificate.

This will just say 'adopted' and will be signed by the registrar who issues the certificate.

If this is the case it is important that you seek advice either from your local Social Services (each authority has a post-adoption worker or special section) or from the adoptions section of the GRO.

England and Wales
Adoptions section
General Register Office
Smedley Hydro
Trafalgar Road
Southport
PR8 2HH
Tel: 0151 471 4830
e-mail: adoptions@ons.gov.uk

Scotland
Adoption Unit
New Register House
Edinburgh EH1 3YT
Tel: 0131 334 0380
(switchboard number ask for adoptions section)
www.gro-scotland.gov.uk
(under 'Registration' there is a link to 'Adoption'.)

Northern Ireland
General Register Office
Oxford House
49-55 Chichester Street
Belfast BT1 4HL
Tel: 028 9025 2000
www.groni.gov.uk/index.htm (follow link for adoption)

Adopted persons may receive help and advice, details about their adoption and support throughout the process of tracing their natural relatives. This service is provided by trained and experienced adoption workers and is free of charge. This will not include a free tracing service but information, counselling and support at every step of the way. If you were adopted it makes sense to use these resources (ideally, this kind of support would be available to everyone seeking a natural relative, whether or not they were adopted. However, it is expensive to run and services are often stretched.)

Agencies and Organisations

The Salvation Army
The well known Family Tracing Service, run by the Salvation Army, was established in 1885. The small unit handles hundreds of enquiries per month and seeks to "restore (or sustain) family relationships, by tracing relatives with whom contact has been lost, either recently or in the distant past."

If your parents were married to each other, this non-profit making service will offer the best value (currently around £35) but may be slow as the demand is high. The Salvation Army will attempt to locate your father and will make contact with him on your behalf. If he is willing they will then put you in touch with each other. They will not give you any details about his location if he does not wish to have contact.

Salvation Army Family Tracing Service
101 Newington Causeway
London SE1 6BN
Tel 0845 634 4747
e-mail: family.tracing@salvationarmy.org.uk
www.salvationarmy.org.uk/en/Departments/FamilyTracing/Home.htm

Traceline

Traceline is a non-profit making government agency operating under the Office for National Statistics. For £30 they will locate a current address for someone in England and Wales who is on a General Practitioner's (doctor's) list. They will also inform you if the person has died or if they are not currently registered with a GP. If a current address is found, they will make a further charge for forwarding a letter (currently £25). Traceline does not reveal any information about the person you are seeking and cannot follow up if no reply is received. Conditions apply and the service is always busy so applications can take several weeks.

Always call in the first instance to discuss whether they can accept your application and to request a form.

> Traceline
> PO Box 106
> Southport
> PR8 2WA
> Tel 0151 471 4811
> **NB** *This service only covers England and Wales. At present there is no similar service for Scotland or Northern Ireland.*

AGRA

The Association of Genealogists and Researchers in Archives is a professional organisation for researchers in England and Wales. By employing a member of AGRA to help you with your search you can be sure that your researcher is experienced, has proven competence when applying for membership, and has agreed to abide by the Association's Code of Practice. Although many members concentrate on family history, some also search for living relatives and a few specialise just in tracing living relatives.

> Joint Secretaries
> AGRA
> 29 Badgers Close
> Horsham
> West Sussex RH12 5RU
> *Find contact details for members on the AGRA web site at* www.agra.org.uk

ASGRA

The Association of Scottish Genealogists and Record Agents is a similar organisation to AGRA covering Scotland. Write for general information (enclose a stamped addressed envelope) or search their web site for a member to help you.

ASGRA,
51/3 Mortonhall Road,
Edinburgh EH9 2HN
www.asgra.co.uk

The Association of British Investigators

It may be more expensive to engage an investigator to undertake your search, but it will possibly be quicker. It is always a good idea to find an investigator who is a member of a professional organisation as they will work to a code of practice.

Some will also work on a 'no find no fee' basis. Be sure to agree a budget before the search commences.

Company Secretary
ABI
48 Queens Road
Basingstoke
Hampshire RG21 7RE
Tel 01256 816390
www.assoc-britishinvestigators.org.uk

Useful web sites

www.192.com

It is not free to search all the data on this web site but the minimum credit purchase of £19.99 is well worth it. 192.com claims to hold electoral register information for 78 million individuals resident in the UK. There is also a CD Rom version available for purchase. You can search by name within a geographical area and unless your father's name is very common or you have no idea of the area he might live in, this can be a very effective search tool. Drawbacks are that you cannot verify who the person is at a given address without making an approach and the data can sometimes be a year or more out of date before it appears on the web site or disc. From 2003 public electoral register entries will be restricted to names of residents who consent to their information being made available.

www.missing-you.net

'The Missing You website offers a free instant on-line message-posting service designed to help enable you to locate missing persons, lost friends, relatives, workmates, forces pals, etc, that are thought to be anywhere in the UK '.

This free service is a way to post details about your dad on the site. It is searchable by name and region but of course depends on the man you are seeking, or someone who knows his current location, reading your message.

www.bt.com/directory-enquiries/dq_home.jsp

The official directory enquires web site from BT. Registration is free and you can search by name and area.

www.genesconnected.co.uk

Established by the team behind the hugely successful Friends Reunited, GenesConnected already boasts over 7 million entries. You will need to register (membership currently £5 per year) to search records. You can e-mail someone from the web site regarding their entry or a person in their family. However, their full name, email address and location are not shown.

Public Records

Electoral Registers

192.com, mentioned above, is a searchable web site of the electoral register. It contains the names of adults in the household who are eligible to vote.

Paper copies of the electoral register, arranged by address only, can be viewed at many local authority offices and public libraries throughout the UK. Authorities collect information from local residents and each area has rules about where the public registers are held and who can view them. Contact the council offices in the area where you think the person lives and ask for electoral registration.

From 2003 public electoral register entries will be restricted to names of residents who consent to their information being made available.

Old electoral registers can be useful too. It doesn't matter if your dad has left the address, even many years ago. The entry for his old address will tell you how long he lived there, what name he was using, his middle initial, who else was resident at the same time and who his neighbours were. This is particularly valuable if your father is not shown on your birth certificate and you are not sure of his full name. If he lived with someone or remarried, his partner's name may also be shown on the electoral register entry for the address. This may make searching for him easier. For example, it can be daunting to look for someone with a fairly common name like Christopher Ward. However, you can narrow down the field considerably if you know that his middle initial is V and that he is now married to a lady called Jennifer.

Former neighbours can be very helpful and may come up with vital information such as the town your dad moved to, the company he worked for or the names and ages of his children.

Birth, marriage and death records
These records, known as civil registration records, are collected by the local register office where the event takes place and then indexed and held centrally by the General Register Office (see above – *How to obtain your birth certificate* – for contact details of the central offices).

Indexes for England and Wales can be searched at the Family Records Centre in London (see below) and at New Register House in Scotland. Here you can find out if someone has married or died, although you will need to order copies of the certificates to obtain full information, which will include their address at the time.

> The Family Records Centre
> 1 Myddelton Street
> London EC1R 1UW
> Tel 0870 243 7788

If you are unable to find any record for your father in the index, searching for the marriage or death of a member of his family may help. The death certificate of his parent will not only give your grand-parent's address at the time of their death but also the name and address of the person who registered the death – usually a close family member.

Wills
If one of your father's parents has died and left a will this is also available to the general public. The contents of a will can be detailed and may give the full names and addresses of all beneficiaries (people who inherited from the deceased). You can apply for a copy

of a will in person at the Principal Probate Registry in London (available to collect the same day) or by post. The cost of a will is currently £5 (cheques payable to HM Paymaster General).

Principal Probate Registry
First Avenue House
42 – 49 High Holborn
London WC1V 6NP
Tel: 020 7947 7000
www.courtservice.gov.uk/cms/wills.htm

Postal applications should be sent, with payment, to –
The Postal Searches & Copies Dept
York Probate Sub-Registry
Duncombe Place
York YO1 7EA
Tel: 01904 666777

Finding your dad through his work
Many professions and occupations have an association or society covering that area of work. Well known examples are the British Medical Association and the Law Society but organisations exist for many professions – architects, electricians, geologists, engineers, interior designers, locksmiths, dentists, vets, physiotherapists etc.
Most of these associations will have a directory of members that may be held at larger libraries or is searchable on the association's web site. There is a very useful book called the Directory of British Associations (published regularly by CBD research) that is stocked my most main libraries. Sometimes a call to the association's headquarters can confirm whether someone is a member, although they may not always be willing to give contact information. However, some organisations may be willing to forward a message or letter to a member.
Company records are covered by data protection laws and will not be given out but again a request to forward a letter or message may be considered.
Company directors must register their full name and home address with Companies House when they submit their annual returns. 192.com has a director search facility or Companies House will be able to tell you if someone is a company director, although there will be a charge for the annual return that will give you his address:

Companies House
Crown Way
Cardiff CF14 3UZ
Tel 0870 3333636
www.companies-house.gov.uk

IMPORTANT NOTE
IF YOU FIND A POSSIBLE ADDRESS FOR YOUR FATHER, DO NOT
ACT ON IMPULSE. READ CHAPTER 2 'MAKING AN APPROACH'
BEFORE TAKING ANY ACTION.

Chapter Two

Making an Approach

First of all, what not to do
If you have found an address for your father think carefully before taking the next step.

You may be impatient after months of searching, you may be desperate to see your father, speak to him, hug him, be angry with him for leaving you, burning with curiosity etc, but to make sure the relationship gets off to a good start – wait! Having an address where your dad lives can arouse overwhelming impulses to just go there, see his house, wait outside, or knock on the door. If you also have a telephone number, just calling to see if he answers, without thinking through exactly what you are going to say, can be a big shock to the person on the other end of the phone.

Put yourself in his position for a moment. You may have spent every waking hour for the last year thinking about meeting your dad, but he may have a completely new life and be in a routine with work, partner and family and possibly have put his past life behind him. That is not to say that he doesn't think about you or wonder how you are getting on but he may not have the need to see you that you have to see him. If a child he last saw thirty years ago suddenly turns up at the door saying 'Hello Dad' this action may sabotage the relationship before it has a chance to get started again. His domestic circumstances may make an approach like this very difficult. He might have a new partner, children who don't know about you, in-laws visiting, builders in the house, his boss on the phone – anything. Similarly, telephoning can be awkward, he may not be home, have had a bad day at work or just need time to think things through before having a conversation with you.

The best way to make an approach to your father is usually by letter.

What to say

What you say if you decide to write depends very much on individual circumstances – yours and his.

If your parents were married and you spent some time with him as a child or have seen him as an adult this may make things easier. It is less likely that you will be a 'skeleton in the cupboard' that might come as a shock to him. In this case it is OK to be open about who you are and why you want to contact him. There may be much you want to say but it's probably best to keep it short initially (see sample letter 1A and 1B).

How do you address him? Only address him as 'Dad' if he was around long enough for you to have called him that before, otherwise the familiarity may make him uncomfortable.

If it is many years since you saw your father or you haven't seen him since you were a baby or your parents weren't married, it's a good idea to be cautious. This is especially true if you think he has remarried or lives with a partner and may have children from later relationships. (see sample letters 2A and 2B).

In some cases the identity of your father may have come only from your mother. It is possible that they separated before you were born or that their relationship was so brief he does not know of your existence. You will need to be especially careful if you intend to contact someone who you think may be your father but you are not sure or have no evidence. Do not assert anything in your initial letter but wait until you can have a conversation before bringing up the subject (see sample letters 3A and 3B).

Sample letter 1A (if you are sure you have the correct address)

Dear Dad
I know it is a long time since we have seen each other and this may come as a surprise to you.
I've been thinking about getting in touch with you for some time and would very much like to know how you are.

The last time I remember seeing you was just after my 14th birthday when you were planning to move to Doncaster to work.

I am working as a shop manager and married Clive three years ago. We have a little girl aged 2 called Sophie. I've enclosed some photographs and would love to see a recent one of you.

Please do get in touch soon.

Best Wishes,

Kate

Sample letter 1B (a speculative letter to a possible address)

Dear Mr Wilson,

I am trying to trace my father, Robert Leslie Wilson. He was born in Glasgow in 1952 and worked in Liverpool between 1973 and 1978. He married my mother, Julianne Clark, in 1974 and I was born in 1976. I was last in touch with him around September 1989 when he was planning to return to Scotland after his mother died. I am therefore writing to everyone called Robert Wilson in the Glasgow area and would very much like to hear from my father. If you are not the same Robert Wilson I'm sorry to have bothered you. Please do let me know that you have received this letter so that I can cross your details off my list. If this letter reaches my father I hope that you are well and would very much like to hear from you.

Yours sincerely,

Celia Wilson

Sample letter 2A (the correct address but unsure of his circumstances)

Dear Mr Jackson,

This may come as a surprise to you as we have not seen each other for many years but I have wanted to get in touch with you for some time.

My name is Mike Norton and I was born in Newcastle in July 1971. My mum (then called Cynthia Turner) lived in Wallace Terrace and remembers you well. She and her friends often wonder how you are. She has shown me some photographs of her with a group of friends and you are in most of them along with Emma Jeeves, Daniel Martin and Steve Nelson.

I'm a keen Internet surfer and I hope you don't mind that looked you up. Although you left the area when I was only seven years old I still remember you. I have just finished university and will be starting work as a trainee chemist next month. I've enclosed a photo me taken in Spain last year.

Please do get in touch soon – I would love to hear from you.

Yours sincerely,

Mike

Sample letter 2B (to a possible address but unsure of his circumstances)

Dear Mr Pearce,

I am trying to contact Jeffrey Pearce formerly from Barnstable as I think it is possible that we may be related. I know that Jeffrey is aged around 51 and his parents were called Frank and Ivy. I am carrying out some research into my family and would very much like to make contact with my Pearce relatives in the area to share historical information and hopefully exchange photographs.

My name is Elizabeth Louise Geary and I am 22 years old – I have enclosed a recent picture. My mum was Charlotte Geary and she lived in Old Factory Road in the 1970s and 80s. She is married and now lives in Cornwall.

If you are not the same Jeffrey Pearce, do let me know so that I can continue my search.

Please get it touch with me soon. I look forward to hearing from you.

Yours sincerely,

Liz Geary

Sample Letter 3A (speculative letter to a possible address)

Dear Mr Jenks,

I am trying to trace a man called Brian Jenks in connection with a possible reunion. Brian is aged around 68 and went to Ealing Technical College, leaving around 1950. Someone who knew Brian at the time is anxious to get in touch with him. If you are the Brian Jenks who went to Ealing College, please can you contact me at the address above or give me a call as soon as you can? If you are not the Brian Jenks described above a quick call or short note to let me know (so that I can cross your details off my list) would be much appreciated. I look forward to hearing from you soon.

Yours sincerely

Cliff Wilkes

Sample Letter 3B (the correct address but unsure if he/his family knows about you)

Dear Mr Edmonds,

I am carrying out some family history research and believe I may have some connection with a family called Edmonds from Rugby.

I wonder if you could possibly get in touch with me soon so that I can establish whether or not we share the same family history? If so I have some information and photographs and would very much like to find out more about your branch of the family. Please can you contact me as soon as possible on the telephone number above?

Many thanks – I look forward to hearing from you soon.

Lydia Mason

These sample letters are just to give you some ideas about what to write and are not necessarily to be used as a template. Don't say anything in your letter that is wildly untrue (although you may need to be 'economical with the truth' at first in order to be discreet), keep it fairly short and leave it up to him to make any return contact. It's probably best not to mention anything about meeting up at this stage. Note that apart from letters 1A and 1B, nothing is mentioned about the man you are writing to being your father. Include full contact details for yourself including address and telephone number and perhaps mobile and email too. You can agonise over what to put in a letter for weeks and will never know if you have said the right or wrong thing until you actually take the plunge and make contact.

Check and double check the address on the envelope before you post it. It is probably best not to use envelopes that are clearly personal stationery – use a plain envelope and write or type the address only without adding 'personal' or 'confidential' as his partner might view this with suspicion. If you feel very nervous about contacting your father direct, think about using an intermediary. This might be an uncle, family friend or trusted professional (e.g. a vicar, doctor or Social Worker) who knows you well and might be willing to make the first approach for you.

Waiting

After sending your letter you may anxiously await the post each morning or jump every time the phone rings for a while. Your father may contact you fairly quickly but it's possible that he may take him some time. Try to be patient as there may be any number of reasons why he doesn't respond immediately. Allow up to around three months before you assume that you are unlikely to hear from him.

If he does get in touch, take things slowly. It is probably best to exchange news and photographs by letter or phone at first. Wait for him to suggest a meeting if you want to take things further.

What to say

It's a good idea to think about what you might say to your father if he calls you, although your mind may go blank when you try to speak to him. Try not to bombard him with questions. He may ask why you have contacted him and if so a low-key response is probably best to begin with. To be confronted immediately with 'I need a dad' or 'I want to meet you' may make him uncomfortable. Alternatively, just asking for a medical history (even if this is one thing that is needed) may make him feel that you are not interested in him as a person. Saying that you have wondered how he is and would like to know what he looks like is a start. Ask him if he wouldn't mind sending a photograph, see how the conversation goes and what his tone is like. You will probably be able to tell after a couple of minutes if he is pleased, responsive, guarded, negative or hostile.

A great response?

It is possible that your father will be overjoyed to hear from you. He may want to have long conversations, hear all about your life, exchange photographs and even meet you straight away. While all of this may feel good, you both need time to get used to the new situation. Even if it is tempting to just meet up, it's probably best to try and take things slowly in the beginning – see 'take your time' below.

Not a good response?

It is a sad fact that some fathers have little interest in their children. Your father may act indifferently or negatively to begin with. If this is the case it is a good idea not to be pushy or make demands, but ensure that he has your contact details and try to get across that you will be pleased to hear from him if he would like to get in touch with you at any time. It is possible that he will come round to the idea of finding out about his child and perhaps getting to know you. If you are desperately in need of a medical history, ask specific questions or write them down and send them to him with a stamped addressed envelope.

Contacting by telephone

Many people find telephone calls intrusive so only consider this option as a last resort if you have written to an address and not received a response.

Be especially careful if it's possible that there are people in the household who might not know about you and anticipate what you might say if someone else answers. If a man picks up the telephone, enquire whether you are speaking with the right person – for example 'Is that Mr Roy Stockard?' If it is, explain that you sent a letter to him at that address several weeks ago and just wanted to check that he has received it. If he says yes but nothing more, he may not want to pursue the conversation at that time. Perhaps reiterate that you would like to hear from him but do not persist in questioning whether he is going to respond – the purpose of the call is just to determine whether your letter reached the right person. If he sounds guarded or uncomfortable you could enquire whether there would be a better time to call, perhaps when he is likely to be alone. Alternatively, it may be more convenient for him to speak with you while at work or on a mobile number so try to be as accommodating as possible.

If you hear nothing

There may be any number of reasons why someone doesn't respond to a letter. It's possible (but unlikely) that the letter was lost in the post and did not arrive.

Maybe the person to whom it was addressed has moved very recently (but is still showing on directories as resident) or is away.

Perhaps the letter arrived at the right address but the man was not the right person and hasn't bothered to respond.

Or maybe he is the right person but for whatever reason (personal circumstances for example) he has decided to ignore the letter.

It can be difficult to accept your father not responding to you, especially if his telephone number is ex-directory you can't call to check that he received your letter. If this is the case it would be acceptable to send just one more short letter (enclosing a stamped addressed envelope) to enquire whether he is still resident at that address and if he received your original letter.

Take your time
Giving your dad time to get used to the idea that you want to see him can help to ensure that when you do meet you are both well prepared. He may need time to absorb information about you, especially if the last time he saw you, you were in nappies and you are now an adult with children of your own. Also, on a practical level he may have a new family. A child from a previous marriage or relationship turning up can cause upheaval in even the most stable household. Telling his partner and children about you might be something he has put off and if so he will need to pick the right moment to do this properly

You might also have plenty to think about and want time to reflect on his life since your separation. Speaking to the people in your life – partner, children, mother, stepfather etc. about what you are doing will hopefully ensure that you have their support throughout.

Getting together

If things go well after your initial approach to your dad, after a while he may suggest you meet up. This might be what you have waited for and to help things go well it is a good idea to plan it carefully.

Where to meet
It will probably be more comfortable for you both if you find a neutral place to meet the first time. He may invite you to his house or you might be eager to show him where you live, but this may put one of you at a disadvantage if you are in unfamiliar surroundings. To make things equal, try to arrange a meeting that is about halfway between where you both live, in a place that is not too isolated nor very public – a park or quiet cafe for example.

It is probably best to meet alone at first. Although you may be desperate to have some moral support, it can be a very private and perhaps emotional event. If you really can't face it alone, ask your partner or a close friend to travel to the meeting place with you, but then it's best if they wander off for a while at the time when you are due to meet your father.

It's a good idea to take along some photographs of yourself over the last few years, and of your partner and children. It is also a good idea to write down a list of questions and keep this in your bag or pocket. You may think of things you wish you had asked only after the event.

Only call him 'dad' if you knew him as a child and have done so before. If not, although he may expect it, it is probably best to ask if he minds or what you should call him.

Try to be friendly and cheerful. Although you might feel that you want to launch yourself into your dad's arms in floods of tears as soon as you see him, he may be more reserved and a little uncomfortable with this. Similarly, this is not the time for angry confrontation or cross-questioning. One young man who at once accused his father of 'not bothering for 26 years' felt very sorry when he was told that his father had suffered an accident 17 years before, resulting in prolonged hospitalisation and severe memory problems. Through rehabilitation and the help of friends from his past the father was finally able to remember his son as a small boy and find the courage to contact him.

Another father had sent cards every birthday and Christmas for 17 years but they had never reached the child – her mother had thought it best that there was no contact and did not give them to her daughter. It is easy to make assumptions but talking about reasons for lack of contact is something that will hopefully come gradually as the relationship develops.

Try to listen as much as you talk and be interested in his life since you last met. Getting to know each other again is a two-way process and it will help make easy conversation if you are both keen to catch up on each other's news.

If you can, set a time in advance for the meeting to finish. Saying 'let's meet for an hour' or 'I have to be home by 3 o'clock' can mean that it is less awkward when it is time to leave. Your head may be spinning after a while and it can be difficult to concentrate or cope with an emotional situation for a prolonged period.

When it is time to leave he may suggest another meeting, this time with other family members. If no suggestion is forthcoming, ask him to keep in touch and perhaps say that it would be nice to see him again. Try not to be pushy about when you will see him again and when he will introduce you to his family. Give him time to get used to having you in his life again. If everything goes well the next step might be a visit to his home, or him coming to visit you, perhaps with his partner and children.

The families

Getting along with your father's partner is the first important part of the equation. She may feel protective of her own position in your father's life and fearful that her children might be neglected.

However strongly you may feel about your right to your father's time and attention, taking into consideration the feelings of family members in his life today can make a positive difference when trying to build a relationship with him.

Be courteous and friendly when you first meet your father's wife or partner. Approval from her can lead to acceptance as a member of the family. Include her in the conversation as much as possible and try not to be too familiar or openly affectionate with your father in her presence at first.

If you have half brothers and sisters from your father's other marriage or relationships, they may or may not have known about you. The sudden introduction of a new brother or sister can be quite a shock, even to an adult. They may be thrilled to meet you and you could get along well from the beginning, but usually there is some caution, even suspicion, of a new sibling. Your introduction to the family may make them feel threatened and insecure resulting in hostility or seeming indifference at first. Rivalry between brothers and sisters is common in all families and sometimes this situation is no different. Even if you have not grown up together, sharing the same father can mean that you unconsciously battle with each other for his attention. Take your time, try to find some common ground and be understanding while they get used to the situation. With younger children it can be easier to win their affection by playing games with them and perhaps giving small gifts (nothing extravagant in the beginning). It can be exciting to have a new big brother or sister but again, if things are difficult at first, try to be patient allow everything to take its own pace.

Little things can help with your acceptance into your dad's new family. Ask the dates of family birthdays and send a card, ask questions about work or school or take along drinks, flowers and sweets for the children when you visit

It can take time, maybe a year or more, before you and your father (and his new family if he has one) feel comfortable with each other. You will gradually work out how often you like to see each other or speak on the phone and how your fit into each others lives. One day, some time after the first meeting, you may feel that you have never been apart.

Hello Dad - Finding your Father

Chapter Four

To DNA or not to DNA?

What is a DNA test?
Before DNA paternity tests, conventional blood tests could some-times provide enough evidence to prove that a man was not the father of a child, or show a high probability that he was the father. Advances in genetic testing in recent years have made DNA testing widely available and affordable to the general public.

DNA is passed down from parents to children. A child inherits one half of his or her genetic makeup from the mother and other half from the biological father. DNA testing can be used to indicate if two children share the same two parents, or if they only have one parent in common.

Moral and ethical issues
As more companies are starting to offer DNA tests, concerns about ethics and procedures have led to the introduction of guidelines, like-ly to become law, to protect the interests of all concerned. Only organisations that comply with the government code of practice will be admitted on to the approved list of testers able to offer DNA paternity tests in the UK.

The 'theft' of DNA for genetic testing looks set to become illegal under the new laws. This means that under no circumstances should a DNA test be conducted without the knowledge and consent of all persons being tested.

Why you might want a test

Just wanting to know may seem reason enough for considering a DNA test to establish for certain if you are someone's child or their biological father.

If there is reasonable cause for doubt (for example if you are unable to ask your mother or if she is not certain who your father is) you may feel that a DNA test is necessary to determine whether or not this man is your father. Similarly, if he is unsure he may request the DNA test to establish his paternity. Sometimes physical similarities are apparent immediately and both of you may feel happy to accept his paternity as fact without any form of test.

If the subject of testing does arise it is important that you should both agree and that the decision to test is a joint one. Before going ahead, consider very carefully why you want the test and discuss between the two of you how you might feel if the results are not as you hope. There can be huge emotional consequences once the results are known and it is something that can never be undone.

Consider also the effect of both a positive and negative result and go ahead only if you are sure that you will be able to cope with either outcome.

Once you decide that you would like to have the test, ensure that you have a good support network to help you cope with any anxiety whilst waiting for the results and also after the results are known. If you have a spouse or partner, talk to them throughout the process and try to ensure that they are with you when you get the results. If you do not have a partner, it may help to talk to other family members, close friends or your doctor about what you are doing and how you are feeling. If necessary, your GP may be able to arrange counselling for you (see also 'useful addresses and sources of support') at the end of the book.

How accurate are the tests?

Paternity tests where the child, mother and father are tested at the same time by the same laboratory usually offer a 99.99 per cent accuracy for a positive test and 100 per cent accuracy for a negative test. Results without a genetic sample from the mother may be slightly less as might results where the father and child were not tested at the same time.

Tests are also available to establish whether someone is your sibling (brother or sister) or half sibling, with or without the father's DNA. Ensure that all parties understand the accuracy of results from this type of test before going ahead.

How to get tested
One way to find out more about DNA testing is to visit your GP. He or she may be able to refer you for a free test or might make recommendations and take samples for you – there may be a charge for this. If you are unable to visit the laboratory in person it is likely that they will ask a trusted authority like a GP to verify that the samples to be tested are from the right person.

The samples can be of blood or cells from the inside of your mouth – a painless test using a mouth swab.

Internet sites offering DNA tests
There are many companies, mostly American, offering DNA testing kits by post. Here you pay by credit card on the Internet, the company sends a kit to all persons being tested, the customers supply their DNA samples using mouth swabs and send them by post to the broker or laboratory. The results are then sent out to everyone tested. This method does not conform to the current Department of Health guidelines on paternity testing for the UK, which states that only the laboratory offering the test, or a health professional, can take the samples to be tested.

Cost of testing
Costs vary between companies and organisations offering DNA testing, but an average amount is around £300 – £400 for a two-person test and £400 – £500 for a three-person (including the mother) test.

Organisations offering DNA paternity testing

University Diagnostics Limited
Tel: 020 8943 7000 (Mondays to Fridays 9am-5.30pm)
www.lgc.co.uk
(go to 'Business Sectors' then 'Consumer Health and Safety' and select 'Paterninty Testing & Relationship Confirmation')
e-mail: udl@lgc.co.uk

Dadcheck
www.dadcheck.com
Tel 0808 145 5789
e-mail: sales@dadcheck.com

Cellmark Diagnostics
PO Box 265
Abingdon OX14 1YX
Tel: 01235 528000
www.cellmark.co.uk
e-mail: cellmark@orchid.co.uk

The Forensic Science Service's Paternity Analysis Unit
Tel: 0121 607 6985 (Mondays to Fridays 8.30am-5.30pm voicemail out of hours)
www.forensic.gov.uk/forensic/entry.htm (follow links from home page through 'Services' then 'Paternity').
e-mail: legalservices@fss.org.uk

Barts and The London – Queen Mary's School of Medicine and Dentistry
Department of Haematology
Dr Denise Syndercombe Court
Turner Street
London E1 2AD
Tel: 020 7377 7076 (Mondays to Fridays 9.30am-5.30pm, plus 24 hour answerphone)
www.smd.qmul.ac.uk
e-mail: y.d.syndercombe-court@qmul.ac.uk

Further reading

Code of Practice and Guidance on Genetic Paternity Testing Services
www.doh.gov.uk/genetics/paternity.htm
Available to download from the Department of Health website.

CSA 2090 (leaflet) – Disputed Parentage and DNA Testing
Information about resolving parentage disputes and DNA testing
Available from the CSA (Child Support Agency) Tel 08457 133 133 or
download from their web site www.csa.gov.uk

Kirby, Lorne T DNA fingerprinting: An introduction Oxford University
Press, 1997 – ISBN 0195118677

Hello Dad - Finding your Father

Chapter Five

Dealing with rejection

Of course everyone hopes for a happy ending when they trace a parent, but sometimes this just doesn't happen. Whatever the reasons for your father not wishing to meet you at this time it is inevitable that you will feel some degree of hurt and rejection. Even if you did not have great hopes for the reunion, the reality of rejection by a parent is hard to take and it feels very personal. Although you may never have met, it can feel as though he doesn't love you or want you in his life because there is something not good enough about you. He is your biological father and if he rejects you it can leave you feeling very small and unloved. However, this is quite unlike being rejected by a lover. He does not know you, so cannot be rejecting you because he doesn't like your habits, faults or personality – the reasons are all his.

Why?
This is the question that comes up when a parent refuses contact and this question will sometimes just not go away. There are a hundred different complex reason why a man does not want to see his child – *none of them are your fault.* Maybe –

The time is not right

He is having a family crisis

He has recently suffered a bereavement

He feels tremendous guilt for leaving your mother or not taking responsibility

His relationship/breakup with your mother was very hard for him feels bitter towards your mother and is worried that she has told you bad things about him

He is worried about the reaction of his partner and other children

The loss of your childhood is too painful for him He is worried about financial implications

He feels that he may not be wanted after the initial meeting

His parents did not know about you and he's worried they will be ashamed He feels that things are 'best left alone'

He is frightened of confrontation and explaining his absence to you

He has personal or health problems

His relationship with his wife/partner may be unstable

......So you see, the possible reasons are endless

What to do
If you receive a negative, indifferent or hostile response to your initial contact, it is possible that this was a 'knee jerk' reaction to the situation on his part. Accept it as that at first, whilst ensuring that your father is aware that you will be happy to hear from him if he changes his mind. Include as many contact details as possible in your initial and any subsequent communication – home, work and mobile telephone numbers, home and work addresses, email and fax. Try to avoid 'pestering' as it may take time for him to think things over and have a change of heart. It may be tempting at this stage to seek him out and confront him face to face, but this is not to be recommended and may make the situation worse. Wait and hope and you may be surprised to hear from your father after a while. If this doesn't happen or you feel that the situation is hopeless, you could send one more *short* letter, asking for his medical history and a photograph (enclosing a stamped addressed envelope). If he refuses to meet you this is perhaps the least he can give, although of course he may also ignore this request.

How to cope

Initially you may feel very upset and although this will subside as time passes it might not disappear completely. Talk through your feelings with your partner, close friends and family members – you may find that they are protective and even indignant on your behalf, which can only help your self esteem at this difficult time. Developing a close relationship with one or two older males, whether they are friends or relatives, so that you have a 'father figure' in your life can also be very comforting. If you have few people in whom you can confide and find that feelings of hurt and rejection are affecting your life, you might consider counselling to help you overcome this. Talking through your thoughts and emotions with a professional can help you to become more objective about the situation and feel more secure. Your GP may be able to arrange NHS counselling for you if your feel very anxious or depressed. Alternatively, contact the British Association for Counselling (details under 'useful addresses and sources of support' at the back of this book) or look in Yellow Pages under 'Counselling and Advice'

Contacting paternal relatives

It is possible that even though your father seems to want no relationship with you, members of his family, who are also *your* relatives, may feel differently. His parents, if they were aware of your birth and are still living, may have longed to see you and might be delighted if you get in touch with them. Your father may also have brothers and sisters – your aunts and uncles – who would be more than happy to hear from you. If your parents were married to each other or in a long-term relationship at the time of your birth you may be confident that his family knows of your existence and perhaps saw you as an infant. If this is the case you could try sending a letter explaining who you are, saying that you would be happy to hear from them and asking to exchange photographs. It may not be a good idea to say anything at first about your father's reaction to your contact. If they are willing to communicate or even meet, try to develop a relationship with them in their own right. Avoid putting them in an awkward position by asking them to speak to your father about the situation or expecting them to take sides. If you are aware, or suspect, that your father's family did not know of your existence the issue is a little trickier. Whether or not it is acceptable for you to get in touch with them, despite your father refusing contact, has no right or wrong answer. Some would argue that his parents, siblings and children are also your blood relatives – you have every right to contact them and they have every right to know about you. The other side of the argument is that if your father himself has refused to have contact with you it would be insensitive, if not selfish of you, to announce your existence to his family regardless. It may also completely sabotage any chance of a relationship with your father in the future. Whatever you decide to do, think carefully, talk it over with trusted people in your life, seek support if you feel that you need it and value yourself despite one man's (perhaps misguided) decision.

Chapter Six

If your father has died

How to find out

If you have searched for a while and have been unable to find your father, at some stage you may begin to suspect that he has died.

To search for a death record in England and Wales you will need to look at the General Register Office index of deaths held at the Family Records Centre in London (address given in chapter 1). Copies of this index are held by some County Record Offices and main public libraries, although they may not be as up to date.

Indexes for Scotland are held at New Register House, Edinburgh and for the General Register Office in Belfast for Northern Ireland records. The indexes are arranged alphabetically by surname. From 1984, these are in one sequence for each year; before 1984 they are arranged by year quarter.

The information given in the index is as follows-

Surname, first names, age at death (and date of birth in post 1984 indexes), district where the death was registered (this is not necessarily the district where the death occurred or where the deceased person lived), month the death was registered (post 1984 only) and reference number (you will need this to order a copy of the certificate).

Death certificates can be ordered in person from the local register office in the district where the person died or from the General Register Office headquarters in Southport (England and Wales), New Register House in Edinburgh (Scotland) or the General Register Office for Northern Ireland in Belfast. Chapter 1 gives contact details and information about how to obtain certificates – this is the same as for obtaining your birth certificate.

Once you have a death certificate and you are certain that it relates to the correct man, take stock before deciding what to do next.

It may be that knowing he has died is enough to lay your curiosity to rest and that you can now get on with your life.

Visiting a significant site
Some people find comfort in visiting a grave, memorial garden or church to bring a sense of closure.

The death certificate gives the deceased person's usual address at the time of death (usually, but not always, the district in which the death was registered).

Almost all local authorities provide what they often call a 'bereavement service' or 'cemeteries department'. They will be responsible for crematoria, cemeteries and co-ordination of bereavement services for the local authority area. The register office or local council can provide contact details for this department. With a deceased person's name and date of death they will be able to inform you whether there is a grave locally, if the grave has a headstone and the exact position within the cemetery. If there is no grave, there may be an entry in the crematorium book of remembrance, or a tree, shrub or stone or bench in a local garden. Visiting the area and even seeing the house your father lived in may make his life seem more real to you. Local libraries often keep archives of newspapers for the area and it is possible that a notice will have been printed in the 'Family Announcements' section.

To see if your father left a will (this would hopefully mention family and friends who benefited from his estate), contact the Courts Service on 0207 947 7000
or visit their web site www.courtservice.gov.uk/cms/wills.htm
for details about how to obtain a will and addresses of local probate offices.

Speaking with his friends and relatives
You may feel desperate to speak with people who knew your father well and to see photographs of him in the years before he died.

Using information from his death certificate, will and any notification in the papers, you can try to locate them using methods described in Chapter 1.

If you think that his family did not know about you and you wish to get in touch with them, approach them sensitively without asserting anything in your initial contact. When you do suggest that their relative may have been your father, they may accept this and want to know more about you. However, be prepared for the possibility of disbelief, denial and even hostility. Present the facts that you are aware of without insisting that he was your father and offer to send them any evidence in the form of photographs, letters or other documents. In time his family will hopefully come round to the idea of having a new relative. See also chapter 6 for ideas about building a relationship with your father's family.

DNA testing if your father is deceased
Even when the suspected biological father is not available, paternity can often be established using paternal relatives. If a man is deceased, samples from his parents (or other relatives) can be used instead. Contact details of DNA testing organisations are given in Chapter 4.

Coping and moving on
Holding the death certificate of your natural father can be a huge emotional blow. Almost inevitably there will be some sadness and grief, although this may take a while to emerge. You may just feel numb, shock or emptiness in the beginning.

Even if you have never known him, you may need to grieve for a relationship that you will never have. As with the situation in chapter 5 where a father has refused contact, developing a relationship with a male 'father figure' such as an uncle, God-parent or older family friend can provide a role model, mentor and mature influence for you and your children.
If you find it hard to cope with the knowledge that your father has died, organisations listed at the end of the book, especially Cruse Bereavement Care (0870 167 1677) and the Samaritans (08457 909090) are there to offer support at this difficult time.

Hello Dad - Finding your Father

Chapter Seven

Real case histories

Names and some details have been changed to protect identities

Caroline's Story

Caroline had always been very curious about her father. She knew that her mum and dad had met at work and that they went out together for about two years. After Caroline was born, her dad saw her a few times but had lost interest in her mum and they drifted apart. He last saw Caroline on her first birthday.

Caroline squeezed every last insignificant piece of information from her mother about her father; What did he look like? How did he speak? What colour were his eyes? What were his likes and dislikes? How did he dress?

She lost sleep through burning curiosity about this man. With two young children and feeling that time was running out she became determined to find him. After a few weeks of trying numbers from the telephone directory she gave up and asked an agency to find him. A month or so later the call came that he had been found. The agency approached him and he wanted to hear from her!

With shaking hands she dialled his number and spoke to a man who sounded much older than she had imagined. 'Is that my daughter?' he asked. She was overjoyed and they had a ten-minute, tearful but joyful conversation. They arranged to meet the following week. On the day of the meeting, Caroline dropped the children at school and drove 20 miles to the teashop where they had planned to meet. She was dressed in her best outfit, had applied her make-up carefully and arrived in plenty of time, with photos of her two young girls ready in her bag.

He was late! Almost 15 minutes after the arranged time he walked in the door and looked around. Caroline had always thought that she would recognise her father instantly if she were to see him but no. He was only 58 but looked ten years older and she could see nothing familiar, nothing of herself in his face. He was affectionate, gave her a gentle hug and greeted her warmly. They ordered lunch and started chatting, hesitantly at first but then more fluently. He asked about her mother – how was she, had she married, what was she doing? He wanted to know about Caroline's children and was complimentary about the photographs she showed him.

Caroline had come prepared with a list of questions, starting with his medical history. Knowing nothing about his health had been a huge disadvantage, particularly during her pregnancies and she had always dreaded medical questionnaires. She was shocked to learn that he had had cancer two years previously but was now in remission. Just after lunch she was also shocked when he lit a cigarette without asking if she minded. As their conversation continued, Caroline started to get slightly bored as he was doing most of the talking, telling her about his job, his new wife, their holidays, his new car and even his garden! 'This is not what I'm here for', she thought, but listened politely. Several times she looked at him and found herself thinking how ordinary he looked. When they parted he promised to send her a photograph of himself and his wife and said that they would see each other again.

The photograph never came, he didn't call and neither did she. However, Caroline noticed one big change in her life – the curiosity had gone. Her lifelong fantasy about her father had disappeared overnight when she met the real, ordinary man. They now exchange Christmas cards and Caroline sends him a family photograph each year but there is little commitment on either side.

'I'm glad I found my dad,' says Caroline, 'because I would always have wondered what he was like. When I saw him he wasn't the man I had imagined at all. He was ordinary, boring and quite selfish. I don't think he's horrible or anything and we will keep in touch, but the reality did not live up to my dream.'

Peter's story

The man Peter had called 'dad' throughout his childhood left the family when he was 14. Peter was not upset, the man had been cruel and there was no bond or affection between them.

'You are old enough to know the truth' said his mother after a few weeks and told him that his real father had been a soldier called Norman who was stationed near their village in Scotland during the war. They had met at a local dance and she had been struck by his good looks and smart appearance. He was friendly and they got talking and then arranged to meet the next night. For several weeks they saw each other as often as they could and he promised to marry her as soon as the war was over. She was completely in love. Soon, however, he was called away to war and then returned to his home in Wales. His letters at first were frequent and full of passion and affection, but as soon as he returned home they became shorter and more reserved and then stopped altogether. Peter's mother had discovered she was pregnant soon after Norman had left and wrote to him with the news. She felt sure that he would return and that they would get married but his letters from Wales did not even have a return address.

After Peter was born her parents supported her and she eventually got a part-time job in a local shop, where she met her husband. Gradually she thought less about Norman but never forgot him and as Peter grew older he became the image of his real father.

Many years later, when Peter was married with grown children, his daughter asked him about her grandfather. He was surprised that he became very emotional when telling her that he had never known his father and had never even seen a photograph of him. Peter's daughter, Kate, resolved to help him to find Norman, but with just a name and only a vague idea of the area where he had lived the task was not easy. With the help of a friend, Kate spent some time at the library looking through telephone directories. This was not working and Kate realised that they could not just call people up and ask if they had got someone pregnant during the war! The right man had to be identified first.

Fortunately, Norman had an unusual surname and Kate decided to look for his birth record. Guessing that he was around 25 at the time of his courtship with her grandmother, Kate found nothing so expanded the search. She found three possible matches making Norman 18, 29 or 32 at the time.

The first one was probably too young, so her grandfather was hopefully going to be one of the other two. As they were both older than she thought, Kate decided to first of all look through death records to see if any of the men had passed away. To her surprise and shock, all three of them had died within the last 15 years. She applied for the death certificates, which gave the names of the family member who had registered the death. In the case of the two older men it was their children and their names and addresses were supplied. Fortunately, they were both still registered to vote at the address given on the certificate, so Kate wrote a short note to each of the relatives saying that she was looking for a man with the same name as their father on behalf of someone who had known him during the war. The son of one man replied to say that his father was never in the armed services even during the war. The daughter of the other man also replied saying that yes, her father had been a soldier, and he had also served in Scotland. Enclosed with the letter was a photograph of a man in uniform, taken around 1944. Peter was stunned – he was the image of this man! He found a picture of himself as a young man and compared the two, then showed them to his wife and daughter. They both wept. Kate was in no doubt that this was her grandfather.

After a week or two when the shock had subsided and he was able to think straight, Peter decided to write to Norman's daughter explaining the situation. A carefully worded letter gave the facts and asked for nothing but a medical history and promised to respect the family if they did not want to acknowledge him. After an agonising wait of over a week, a hostile and indignant letter was received from Norman's daughter – how dare they suggest that her father was unfaithful, what proof could they offer, this was an outrage etc. Peter was left in no doubt that further contact would not be welcome and reluctantly resigned himself to never knowing the truth, although secretly he was fairly certain that he had identified the right man. He hoped that Norman's daughter would have a change of heart and wrote once more a few weeks later but never heard from her again. After three months Peter made a visit to Norman's grave and described this as 'a very emotional day'. He still treasures the photograph, sure in his own mind that he now knows who is father was.

Anna's story

When Anna decided to look for her father, she never could have known the difficulties that lie ahead and admits now that she sometimes wishes she had never started the search for him. Anna knew, however, that her father, Malcolm, had loved her and wanted very much to keep her and this is what made her decide to go ahead with the search.

Anna's parents had separated when she was three years old and she remained with her mother only after a fierce custody battle. Her mother remarried when Anna was five and the new family moved to Ireland to start a new life. Although she was happy, she always knew she had another father.

At the age of 45, married to Ian and with three children, she decided that the time had come to look for her father as she was between jobs and had spare time on her hands. After a few weeks searching marriage records and making dozens of phone calls she eventually had the correct address and decided to write a short letter telling her father who she was and that she would like to hear from him.

The next morning the telephone rang and a shaky voice enquired if she was Anna. When she replied yes, her father wept with joy and they spoke on the telephone for over an hour. They seemed to get along so well that after just one week and many more emotional calls they decided that she must visit. Malcolm's wife, Gillian, was very understanding and had known about Anna for many years. Their children, Marcus and Elaine, also seemed to take things well. Arriving at the railway station after a long journey from Ireland to the north of England, Anna was delighted that the whole family had come to meet her. She fell into her father's arms and they hugged for a long time.

Introductions were made they had a pleasant day getting to know each other. After two days Anna had to leave but her father made her promise to return again soon and to bring her family with her.

Anna was ecstatic and when she arrived home couldn't stop talking about how wonderful Malcolm was. They spoke on the telephone daily and wrote each other long, affectionate letters. Three weeks later she returned to visit him again, this time taking her husband and the two youngest children with her. Everything seemed perfect – the children were greeted fondly and Anna sat for many hours with her father.

The first sign that something might be wrong came when Marcus refused to join them for Sunday lunch. He was 'being a bit funny about everything' said Malcolm. Anna noticed that Gillian seemed to be reluctant to leave her alone with Malcolm and had become a little less friendly towards her, but Ian said she seemed fine to him and suggested that perhaps Anna should not be so physically affectionate to her father as it might cause some jealousy. She and Ian argued and struggled to maintain appearances for the rest of the visit. Things very quickly moved from bad to worse. Although she and her father continued to speak daily and remained as committed to the relationship as ever, everyone around them seemed to be growing increasingly resentful of their closeness.

Malcolm visited Anna alone for a few days the following month and said that things were 'not good' between him and Gillian. She was most alarmed to receive a spiteful call from Marcus telling her to leave his father alone and this was followed by a letter from Gillian pleading with her to stop trying to destroy their marriage. She could not stop calling her father – he had become her best friend – and Malcolm told her that having lost her once he was not about to let her go again.

Ian become increasingly resentful of the time Anna spent speaking with, or about, her father, and their relationship became strained. Finally, five months after they had first met, Malcolm visited Anna and told her that his marriage was over. Gillian could no longer accept that she and her children were not Malcolm's first priority. Marcus made abusive calls to Anna and Elaine refused to speak to her. Ian was unsupportive and became withdrawn. Malcolm and Gillian divorced but slowly the relationship between Anna and her husband improved. He agreed, after much discussion, to allow Malcolm to live with them for a while until he could rebuild his life. At the time of writing, Malcolm is divorced, has moved into a flat near Anna and has a new lady friend. Anna and Ian have re-established their happy marriage and see Malcolm regularly but Malcolm's ex-wife and other children are not in contact with him or Anna.

Joanna's story

Joanna had never got along well with her mother, Sandra, and it did not help that she was never told about her father. Sandra described him as a 'one-night stand' and Joanna only knew that his name was Ron. This information had come from her Auntie Jean as her mother refused to discuss their relationship or tell Joanna anything about him.

Working as an air hostess meant that Joanna had little time for research and she did not yet feel ready to buy a home of her own as she was away so often. She moved in with her aunt as a temporary measure, but the situation worked well for both of them and she stayed.

After her mother's death, Joanna decided that now was the time to look for her dad and grilled Auntie Jean for more information. She found out that her parents had lived together for about six months and that Ron was already married at the time. When he discovered that Sandra was pregnant he returned to his wife and Sandra never saw him again. Joanna's birth certificate did not give a father's name but Jean remembered that his surname was Bignell.

A search of marriage records showed a Ronald Bignell getting married in the right area four years before Joanna's birth and she applied for the certificate. Ronald's occupation, according to the marriage certificate, was 'Chartered Surveyor'. This matched what Jean remembered about him and Joanna was sure this man was her father. She visited the library and looked in the latest directory of Chartered Surveyors and found that Ronald Bignell was still listed as practising, not far from where he had lived with her mother.

Joanna called his office but was told that Mr Bignell had retired three months previously but a quick search of the electoral register for the area gave her his home address.

She sat down to compose a letter, which took many hours. Eventually, a short note explaining who she was and asking him to contact her was despatched with high hopes. Joanna heard nothing for over a week and then left on a four-day trip to New York. Whilst she was away, Ron telephoned her aunt asking 'What does she want?' Jean tried to explain that as Sandra had died, Joanna really wanted to know a little bit about her father. Ron replied briskly that 'her letter could have caused a lot of trouble' and Jean gathered that Ron's wife did not wish to be reminded of her husband's infidelity. Ron asked Jean to tell Joanna to 'forget it'.

Joanna was obviously very upset when she returned to this news and at first felt like going straight to his house to confront him. However, she realised that this would be counterproductive. She tries hard to remain optimistic that Ron will eventually change his mind and keeps busy with her work but still feels that something is missing from her life.

Cliff's story

Cliff says that the day he spoke with his father again after 29 years was the best day of his life.

Cliff's mother and his father, Richard, had divorced when Cliff was five. His father was in the Navy and away at sea regularly. There were vague memories of a large man in uniform with sandy hair carrying him, a few photographs of his parent's wedding day and just one picture of baby Cliff in his father's arms. Cliff is a successful software designer and after four years of marriage and two lovely children, he decided that he would very much like to see his father again.

Cliff's mother was helpful and told him everything she could remember about Richard and his family. He had been an only child and his parents, Margaret and Harold Newman, lived in Peterborough. Cliff searched the Internet directories for his father but there were too many people of the same name to attempt contacting them all. He looked for Harold and Margaret, his grandparents and did find a Margaret Newman living in the right area. Unsure of what to do next, Cliff left things for a while. Four months later, a business trip led him past Peterborough and this prompted him to pay a visit to the address where this Margaret Newman was registered to vote.

Expecting a frail old lady, Cliff was surprised to find a young looking 70 year old lady planting flowers in the front garden. He asked if she was Mrs Newman and she started to reply, but looking up at him she suddenly exclaimed 'I know who you are!'

She was indeed his grandmother and she was overjoyed to see him. She invited him in, hugged him, cried and told him how she had thought about him and missed him over the years. Cliff was surprised to see a picture of himself aged about three years old sitting on a shelf in Margaret's living room. Over a cup of tea, Cliff was told how Richard had settled in New Zealand after leaving the Navy 15 years earlier. Margaret had nagged him to keep in touch with Cliff. Richard had always intended to, but was busy with a new wife and twin sons, now aged 14.

Margaret promised to call Richard and let him know that Cliff had made contact so Cliff left feeling very happy.

When he arrived home the next day, his wife told him that his father had called and wanted to hear from him. Nervously, Cliff dialled the number. Richard answered and they had a long, easy conversation. Richard's wife, Julie, had known about Cliff all along and the twins had been told about their 'big brother in England' several years ago.

Richard had always intended to find Cliff and was planning a trip to England the following year.

Richard and Cliff share an interest in computers and kept in touch by email, also exchanging family pictures. Ten months after Cliff first called on his grandmother, he, Margaret and Richard sat together in the same room and talked for hours while their families got to know each other. Cliff gets along well with his half brothers, and feels very close to his dad. It was very hard to say goodbye. He is planning a visit to New Zealand in two years and can't wait. In the meantime, however, there is always email and a huge phone bill. As Cliff describes the situation 'Things couldn't be better!'

Maria's story

Maria had been adopted as a baby and was now married with two children. She had already found a great deal of information about her mother and traced her three sisters. Maria's mother had died when Maria was just a baby of 19 months and all three sisters had been taken into care shortly after as their father was unable to cope. Maria had been adopted, the next sister was placed with a foster family and stayed with them for a number of years but the two older girls went together to a children's home. All four sisters were reunited shortly after Maria turned 30 – they had all been looking for each other! Maria was most keen to find their father, as she did not remember him at all. She had details from her adoption file and set about trying to locate him, with the help of an agency.

Maria's father was found quite quickly and she wrote a letter to him, but asked her local vicar to send it and gave only his address and telephone number. The letter was posted on a Friday and he telephoned the very next morning, delighted that his daughter wanted to get in touch. They spoke at length soon afterwards. Her father sounded nice but said that he was lonely since the death of his second wife. He wanted Maria to send photographs of herself and her family immediately and was soon asking if he could visit her.

The first visit went well – he bought expensive presents for the whole family and asked them to come and stay with him for a weekend, which they did. But soon Maria began to find his attention a little suffocating and was most uncomfortable when, within two months of their first contact, he wept that she was now his only reason for living. Gradually she managed to 'cool things down' without hurting his feelings and introduced him to two of his other daughters (the eldest did not want to meet him).

After a year of fairly regular visits and phone calls, Maria and her family moved to France. They remain in contact with her father and he has visited once, but is reluctant to travel too often. Maria describes the situation now as 'just right'. She and her father write about once a month, send each other birthday and Christmas cards and speak on the phone maybe two or three times a year. She is pleased that she found her father and now feels 'complete'.

Useful addresses and sources of support

British Association for Counselling and Psychotherapy
The BAC can provide a list of private counsellors in your area, plus information on counselling and choosing a counsellor. Telephone or send an SAE to the above address. The BAC web site also has an online directory of approved counsellors, searchable by geographical area.
BACP House
35-37 Albert Street
RUGBY
CV21 2SG
0870 443 5252 (Mondays to Fridays 8.45am-5pm)
e-mail: bacp@bacp.co.uk
www.counselling.co.uk
Your GP will also be able to give advice about counselling sources locally.

National Association of Citizens Advice Bureaux
The CAB provide advice and information on paternity testing, tracing missing persons and how to obtain counselling. Details of local Citizen's Advice Bureaux are available on the website or in your local telephone directory.
www.nacab.org.uk
Try looking for an online news or self help group at groups.google.com/

Parentline Plus
This organization provides information and support to families.
It operates a national free phone telephone helpline. Parentline Plus
520 Highgate Studios
53-79 Highgate Road
London NW5 1TL
Tel: 020 7284 5500
Helpline 0808 800 2222
www.parentlineplus.org.uk/templates/home/index.cfm

Families Need Fathers
This organisation offers support for fathers who are living apart from their children.
Their web site has useful links.
Families Need Fathers.
134 Curtain Road,
London EC2A 3AR
Tel/fax: 020 7 613 5060
Helpline: 020 8295 1956 / 01920 462 825
www.fnf.org.uk/

The **Samaritans** offer someone to talk to 24 hours a day
www.samaritans.org.uk/
or call 08457 909090 for confidential emotional support.

Cruise Bereavement Care
Support when you lose a loved one and publications
about losing a parent to help you cope .
www.crusebereavementcare.org.uk
or telephone 0870 167 1677

Printed in the United Kingdom
by Lightning Source UK Ltd.
99066UKS00001BA/15-116